James

Lehman Strauss

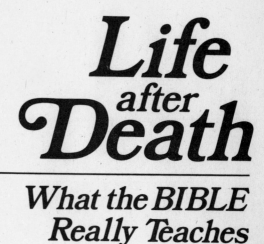

Life
after
Death

What the BIBLE Really Teaches

ONE EVENING
CHRISTIAN
CLASSICS®

Good News Publishers
Westchester, Illinois

A *One Evening Christian Classic*™
Published by Good News Publishers,
Westchester, Illinois 60153.

An abridged edition of the
original Christian classic
first published by Loizeaux Brothers
in 1947 under the title *We Live Forever*,
copyright © Lehman Strauss.
Produced by special arrangement
with the original publisher.

This printing, 1982.

Contents

CHAPTER ONE

Death

The Certainty of Death

The valley of the shadow of death is the longest valley in the world. It began with Adam and has continued through six thousand years of human history. Men like to postpone that dreadful moment when they must pass through the dark valley, but death underscores each life and refuses to accept the person of any man. Death does not take into account whether we have been profitable or detrimental to society. Every step that we take brings us nearer to the grave, and it is but a matter of time until we must bid farewell to every earthly tie. With all of the wisdom of the medical profession and the use of scientific discoveries, we must agree with the wise preacher of old who said: "For the living know that they shall die" (Ecclesiastes 9:5).

The Bible contains much warning about death, speaking as frequently on this subject as it does about any other. In the garden of Eden where death had never entered, Adam and Eve were instructed by God to refrain from the forbidden fruit with the accompanying warning:

"In the day that thou eatest thereof thou shalt surely *die*" (Genesis 2:17).

We know that they did eat; and at the very moment the judgment of God passed upon them, their bodies commenced the process of death and decay. "And all the days that Adam lived were nine hundred and thirty years: *and he died*" (Genesis 5:5).

The Patriarchs, Prophets, and Apostles did not hesitate to declare that death is certain. Noah preached righteousness and the judgment of God. He warned men that if they would not repent, the Lord would destroy them from the face of the earth (Genesis 6:7). Men only mocked at the old preacher's sermon, and then God struck the whole earth with death and destruction. The divine record has it that the waters prevailed for forty days on the earth until every hill was covered. And then we read:

> "*And all flesh died* that moved upon the earth, both of fowl, and of cattle, and of beast, and of every creeping thing that creepeth upon the earth, *and every man*" (Genesis 7:21).

Abraham faced the grim reality of death when he offered Isaac as a sacrifice to the Lord. Though Isaac was spared, a ram died in his stead. Then we read: "*And Sarah died*" (Genesis 23:2).

When Jesus told the story of the rich man and Lazarus, He said:

> "The beggar *died*... The rich man also *died*" (Luke 16:22).

When Christ was brought before the multitude, the Jews said:

> "We have a law, and by our law He ought to *die*" (John 19:7).

Of Dorcas, Luke writes:

> "She was sick, and *died*" (Acts 9:37).

How full the Bible is of the subject of death! We cannot study the life of any Bible character, save Enoch and Elijah, without being reminded that they all died. Life insurance companies become rich simply by pointing out that all men must die, and the agents have little difficulty in selling a policy by merely stating that death may come suddenly and unexpectedly. Any undertaker who conducts a respectable business is assured of a comfortable living with those values that money can buy. Even architects and builders take death into account when they plan a structure. Dr. John Rice tells that when his congregation in Dallas was preparing plans for a new church building the architect insisted on discussing the stairways, for, said he: "One rule we architects try to remember is that every stairway and every bedroom door must be large enough to admit a coffin!"

The Bible speaks of

"The law of sin and *death* (Romans 8:2).

The Apostle Paul says:

"We had the sentence of *death* in ourselves" (2 Corinthians 1:9).

"So then *death* worketh in us" (2 Corinthians 4:12).

The Epistle to the Hebrews speaks of men

"Who through fear of *death* were all their lifetime subject to bondage" (Hebrews 2:15).

The Cause of Death

God never acts in judgment nor does He allow anything to come to pass unless there is a just cause. So when He pronounced death upon the human race it was because Adam and Eve had disobeyed God and turned from the truth. Though the warning of the Lord had come in soundness and simplicity man chose to sin, knowing all the while that it meant death. Man cannot plead innocency on the ground of the sovereignty of God. He is appointed to die because he has transgressed the Law of God, and the Lord's justice in the sentence of death is so undeniable that every mouth is stopped and all the world is guilty before Him. Man can offer no legitimate reason why the death sentence should not have been passed, for

"The wages of sin is death" (Romans 6:23).

"The soul that sinneth, it shall die" (Ezekiel 18:4).

"Sin, when it is finished, bringeth forth death" (James 1:15).

"By one man sin entered into the world, and death by sin" (Romans 5:12).

"So then death worketh in us" (2 Corinthians 4:12).

"For all have sinned" (Romans 3:23).

The Course of Death

Death does not affect all men in the same way simply because it does not lead all men in the same direction. In one hospital ward two patients may die at exactly the same moment. While the root cause of these deaths may be the same in each case, the dying of one can be something altogether different from the dying of the other. We have seen how that death was the only punishment for sin that could satisfy the righteous demands of God. Since all men possess Adam's fallen nature, it stands that all must die the physical death of the body. However, as Abraham Kuyper has said: "In the valley of the shadow of death, the great highway on which people walk divides itself, and continues on one side upward unto eternal life, and on the other with a declining path downward into eternal death."

We can understand this only as we know something of the true purpose of the death of Jesus Christ. Since sin must be punished by death, Jesus went to the cross and died as the punishment for sin and thus at the same time offered Himself as the satisfaction for sin. Peter declares that "Christ also hath once suffered for sins, the just for the unjust, that He might bring us to God, being put to death in the flesh" (1 Peter 3:18). Here we are told that Christ was put to death for sins "that He might bring us to God." Those who fall asleep in the Lord take the upward course to Heaven and to God. We were, by nature, on the downward course, doomed to be separated from God; but Jesus, by His death, provided a new destiny.

Since the death of Christ paid for the believer the punishment of sin, and death to him is a pleasant ascension into the Father's presence, it follows that the death of the unbeliever is an unpleasant descent away from the presence of God. When the unbeliever gives up the ghost, breathing his last breath, he passes from this world into a spiritual and eternal death and Hell. Both are conscious, but death was forced to pursue a different course for each.

Dear reader, where are you? Yes, you are still alive in this world; but remember, death is slowly but surely overtaking you. Soon you must say farewell to every earthly tie and enter into an endless eternity. Since Christ died to bring you to God, it is self-evident that you are far from God, and un-prepared and unfit for Heaven. Will you trust the Saviour now? "He that believeth not shall be damned" (Mark 16:16).

CHAPTER TWO

Man a Trinity—Spirit, Soul, Body

The Christian doctrine of immortality cannot be under-stood apart from the right conception of the tripartite nature of men. Many think that man is a physical being only. There is a great danger of any man thinking thus of himself. In his desire to satisfy the needs of the body there is the tendency on man's part to lose sight of the fact that he is immortal. There have been persons who have lived all their lives either in ignor-ance or willful neglect of a life after death, but upon their death-bed they suddenly realized that they were more than physical beings.

The two following passages from the Bible clearly establish the fact that man is composed of spirit, soul, and body—

"I pray God your whole *spirit* and *soul* and *body* be pre-served blameless unto the coming of our Lord Jesus Christ" (1 Thessalonians 5:23).

"For the word of God is quick, and powerful, and sharper than any two edged sword, piercing even to the dividing as-under of *soul* and *spirit*, and of the *joints* and *marrow* (body), and is a discerner of the thoughts and intents of the heart" (Hebrews 4:12).

The Bible states emphatically that man was created a trinity of spirit, soul, and body even as the eternal God is Himself a trinity of Father, Son, and Holy Ghost. The trinity of man is an essential part of the image relationship between him and God. Life is not ultimately physical and the body is not the whole man.

The Spirit.

The spirit of man, being the sphere of God-consciousness, is the inner or private office of man where the work of regener-

ation takes place. Dr. James R. Graham says that the main
theatre of the Holy Spirit's activity in man, and the part of
man's nature with which He has peculiar affinity, is *the spirit
of man*. The Apostle Paul gives us the Word of God on this,
a passage that is sadly neglected. Quoting from the sixty-
fourth chapter of the book of the Prophet Isaiah, Paul wrote:

> "But as it is written, Eye hath not seen, nor ear heard,
> neither have entered into the heart of man, the things which
> God hath prepared for them that love Him."

A great many people stop here, content to remain in ignorance.
However, Paul continues:

> "But God hath revealed them unto us by His Spirit: for the
> Spirit searcheth all things, yea, the deep things of God.
>
> "For what man knoweth the things of a man, save the spirit
> of man which is in him? even so the things of God knoweth
> no man, but the Spirit of God" (1 Corinthians 2:9-11).

Man in his unregenerate state comes to know the things
of man by the operation of "the spirit of man" which is in him.
If I have a will to know certain facts, by my human spirit I
am enabled to investigate, think, and weigh evidence. However, my human spirit is limited to "the things of man." If
I want to know about the things of God, my dead and dormant
spirit is not able to know them—

> "The natural man receiveth not the things of the Spirit of
> God: for they are foolishness unto him: neither can he know
> them, because they are spiritually discerned" (I Corinthians
> 2:14).

The human spirit requires "the spark of regeneration" before there is an understanding of the things of God. Man's
spiritual nature must be renewed before there is a true conception of godliness. Only one thing stands as a guard at the
door of man's spirit, and that is his own *will*. When the will
is surrendered, the Holy Spirit takes up His abode in the spirit
of man. And when that transaction takes place we will know
it, for, says Paul:

> "The Spirit Himself (meaning the Holy Spirit) beareth wit-
> ness with our spirit, that we are children of God" (Romans
> 8:16 R.V.).

Many people confess that they get nothing out of the Bible even though they attend church and read their Bibles regularly. Perhaps they do not know that they are not regenerated and that they need to yield their will to the Spirit of God so that He can renew their human spirits. The deep things of God never will be understood by the world outside of Jesus Christ. Our Lord warned His disciples,

"Give not that which is holy unto the dogs, neither cast ye your pearls before swine" (Matthew 7:6).

The spirit of the unregenerate man has no more capacity to appreciate the things of God than a dog has to appreciate holy things, or a hog a genuine pearl necklace. We read that "The dog is turned to his own vomit again; and the sow that was washed to her wallowing in the mire" (2 Peter 2:22). This they did because the dog was a dog and the sow was a sow. No amount of religion or church activity can change the spirit of the unregenerate man. "Remember," says Dr. G. Campbell Morgan, "if out of false charity or pity you allow men of material ideals and worldly wisdom to touch holy things, to handle the pearls of the Kingdom, presently they will turn and rend you. That is the whole history of Christendom's ruin, and the measure in which Christendom is ruined. We gave holy things to dogs. We cast the pearls of the Kingdom before swine." The ministry of Christ's Church dare not be entrusted to any man who has not been born again, for "That which is born of the flesh is flesh; and that which is born of the Spirit is spirit" (John 3:6)

The Bible says: "There is a Spirit in man: and the inspiration of the Almighty giveth them understanding" (Job 32:8). Here we are told that it is the spirit of man that is given understanding. The materialist tells us that the spirit of man is the air that he breathes, and that man's body is all there is to his personality. Such is not the case. The spirit of man is his personality and it is that which differentiates him from the lower animal creation. If "spirit" meant merely "breath," God certainly would not deal with it as a personality. He is called

"The God of the spirits of all flesh" (Numbers 16:22), and "the Father of spirits" (Hebrews 12:9). It is by his spirit that the Christian both serves and worships God. Paul testified: "For God is my witness, Whom I serve with my *spirit* in the Gospel" (Romans 1:9). Jesus said: "God is a spirit: and they that worship Him must worship Him in *spirit* and in truth" (John 4:24).

The Soul

Man not only has a living soul but he *is* a living soul. The Bible says: "And the Lord God formed man of the dust of the ground, and breathed into his nostrils the breath of life, and man became a living soul" (Genesis 2:7). We must be careful not to confound that which is truly spiritual and that which is merely soulish or psychical. We have seen that the spirit of man is the sphere of activity where the Holy Spirit operates in regeneration. Just so is the soul the sphere of activity where Satan operates making his appeal to the affections and emotions of man.

The soul of man, that is, his affections and desires, are never directed Godward until after the spirit has become regenerated. Man can never love God nor the things of God until he is born from above. He may have a troubled conscience or be so stirred emotionally that he may weep bitterly, and still remain dead in trespasses and in sins. Man's desires and affections are turned toward God when he realizes his sinful condition and God's grace in salvation. When the Spirit of God illuminates the spirit of a man with divine light and life, that man begins to yield his affections and faculties to God.

In that immortal classic of the Psalms, David says: "He restoreth my soul" (Psalm 23:3). The Hebrew word translated "restoreth" is said to mean quite literally "turneth back." At no time had David lost his salvation, but there were times when his affections and desires were turned from the Lord, as in the case of his sin with Bathsheba. Having become one of the Divine Shepherd's flock, he testified: "The Lord turneth back my soul." The Christian who is enjoying unbroken communion with his Lord will then be able to say, "Bless the Lord, O my soul: and all that is within me, bless His holy name" (Psalm 103:1).

CHAPTER THREE

Can We Believe In Immortality?

The Witness of the Ancients

The word immortal means exemption from liability to death. That which is immortal is not liable to death.

Wherever death has come it seems to have brought with it a conscious assurance of immortality. The immortal soul of saint and savage has voiced a hope in life beyond the grave.

Egypt, the classroom of the world's finest arts and sciences, had a strong faith and a feeling of certainty in immortality. Their conception of a future life originated the idea and construction of the pyramids, one of the wonders of the world.

The heathen of Africa believe in life after death. We are told that the wives of the deceased take up their residence near the tomb so that they can remain the rest of their earthly lives "to watch the departed spirit." In some ancient Asiatic tribes the belief was held that the next world could be reached by the cremation of the body, the fire god taking the deceased to the gods of the other world. Sometimes animals were sacrificed in the fire to precede the corpse to the land beyond.

Through six millenniums of human history man has looked upon immortality as a reality. Universally believed, it is the most indestructible of all instincts and the most penetrating of all intuitions. We agree with Dr. Lockyer when he said: "Without hesitation, affirm that the belief in a future state was derived from a revelation made to our first parents by their Creator, and that it travelled down the ages. The Hope of Immortality, resident within the breast of both savages and saints, was planted there by Him who has no beginning or end."

The Witness of The Bible

When we approach the Bible on the subject of immortality, it is well to have in mind a few important facts that are basic and necessary to a proper understanding of the subject. Nowhere in the Bible is the expression to be found, "the immortality of the soul." Nor is there written anything about "the immortal soul." We are not suggesting for a moment that Scripture teaches anything about the sleep or annihilation of the soul at death. The thought of the soul's endless being is true enough, but it is not Scriptural language to refer to "the immortality of the soul." The Word of God assumes the eternal existence of every soul regardless of its destiny. Every man's soul is immortal and can never be annihilated. Jesus said: "Fear not them which kill the body, but are not able to kill the soul: but rather fear him which is able to destroy both soul and body in Hell" (Matt. 10:28).

Three Kinds of Death

It is true we read: "The soul that sinneth, it shall die" (Ezekiel 18:4), but neither here nor elsewhere in Scripture does a reference to the soul dying mean a state of non-existence, or even one of unconsciousness. The Bible teaches that there are three kinds of death and it distinguishes clearly between each. First, there is physical death, or the separation of the soul from the body. This is the death of the body to which reference was made in Hebrews 9:27, "It is appointed unto men once to die." Second, the Bible teaches that there is a spiritual death. This is the separation of the soul from God, the condition of all unbelievers of whom Paul says they are "dead in trespasses and sins" (Ephesians 2:1), and "alienated from the life of God" (Ephesians 4:18). Third, there is eternal death or banishment from God. All who suffer eternal death are conscious, but "shall be punished with everlasting destruction from the presence of the Lord" (2 Thessalonians 1:9), these "have their part in the lake which burneth with fire and brimstone: which is the second death" (Revelation 21:8).

The Immortal Becomes a Mortal

The words "immortal" and "immortality" when used in Scripture in reference to man find their application to the body. The body of our first parent, as God created him, was an immortal body created to endless existence. God had warned Adam and Eve against eating the fruit of the tree of the knowledge of good and evil, saying: "In the day that thou eatest thereof thou shalt surely die" (Genesis 2:17). They disobeyed, and immediately death began its work in the body. The immortal had put on mortality. Paul says: "Wherefore, as by one man sin entered into the world, and *death by sin*" (Romans 5:12). So then, says the writer to the Hebrews, "It is appointed unto men once to die" (Hebrews 9:27).

Deliverance From Mortality

The purpose of the coming of our Lord Jesus Christ was to offer redemption to the fallen race. No mortal could have done this. The dead cannot impart life. The only way that man could escape the sentence of death was by "the appearing of our Lord Jesus Christ. . . . Who only hath immortality" (1 Timothy 6:14, 16). The soul of man, though retaining endless existence, became morally degenerate. After the fall, his body became corruptible, and his spirit lost all relationship with God. But a glorious truth is given us by the Apostle Paul. He says: "The appearing of our Saviour Jesus Christ, hath abolished death, and hath brought life and immortality to light through the gospel" (2 Timothy 1:10). O wondrous thought! The Immortal One became mortal, "obedient unto death (Philippians 2:8), that He might redeem man's soul, restore his spirit to right relation with God and make his body heir to incorruptibility. This is the triumph of the cross of Christ. By His death and resurrection from the grave our Lord "abolished death." He was willing to be clothed with mortality "that through death He might destroy him that had the power of death, that is, the devil" (Hebrews 2:14). "For as in Adam all die, *even so in Christ shall all be made alive*" (1 Corinthians 15:22).

Eternal Life and Immortality

It seems to the writer that the subject under consideration is made clearer as we see a difference between eternal life and immortality. The terms are not synonymous. The moment one trusts Jesus Christ for salvation he receives everlasting life. This is God's gift bestowed to the sinner upon his acceptance of Jesus Christ as his own personal Saviour from sin. "He that believeth on the Son hath everlasting life" (John 3:36). "He that believeth on Me hath everlasting life" (John 6:47). "But these are written, that ye might believe that Jesus is the Christ, the Son of God; and that believing ye might have life through His Name" (John 20:31). The glorious work of redemption for sinners is effective in any individual just as soon as he is born again, but it cannot be correctly stated that at that moment the soul became immortal. As a matter of fact the soul never lost its immortality. Regeneration by the Holy Spirit is but the beginning of the redemptive process. Immediately upon the Holy Spirit's taking residence in man's spirit, the soul receives eternal life. But the body, even though it has become heir to immortality and incorruptibility, must die. The only possibility the Christian has of his body escaping death and the grave is the return of Christ to rapture all believers to Himself. It follows then that one can possess and enjoy eternal life while death and the grave stare him in the face.

The Apostle Paul says: "We ourselves groan within ourselves, waiting for the adoption, to wit, the redemption of our body" (Romans 8:23). But is there any guarantee that this corruptible body will put on incorruption? Can we be certain that the mortal will one day be clothed with immortality? We only say that in order to fulfill the redemption covenant and promise, Jesus Christ is under oath and obligation to raise the bodies of all the dead who died trusting in Him. There is bright hope and full assurance in the words of our Lord: "I am the resurrection, and the life: he that believeth in Me, though he were dead, yet shall he live" (John 11:25). Our Lord's own testimony assures us of the deliverance from death and decay to life and immortality.

The redemption of the soul is past, but the redemption of the body is still future. Since man is a trinity, and all three component parts of him must be united, it can only be possible as man is restored once again to the image and likeness of God. This is exactly what takes place at the resurrection "when man—the unit—with his tripartite nature is reconstructed into an immortal." The Gospel did not have its consummation with the death of Christ. Paul said: "I declare unto you the Gospel...how that Christ died for our sins according to the Scriptures; and that He was buried, and that He rose again the third day according to the Scriptures" (1 Corinthians 15:1-4). Jesus Christ the Immortal One, became mortal by His death. But it was only temporary mortality. By His resurrection from death and the grave to immortality, the Son of God guarantees the same for all that are His. By the first Adam came mortality and death, and by the Last Adam came life and immortality. "Now is Christ risen from the dead, and become the firstfruits of them that slept...But every man in his own order: Christ the firstfruits; afterward they that are Christ's at His coming" (1 Corinthians 15:20, 23). As every child of Adam dies, so will every child of God be raised never to die again.

"They that are Christ's" tells us who shall become immortal. "At His coming!" This tells us when we shall become immortal. Immortality is the final step of redemption when our Lord comes again. It is for the redeemed only, for even as "flesh and blood cannot inherit the kingdom of God; neither doth corruption inherit incorruption" (1 Corinthians 15:5).

"The dead shall be raised incorruptible, and we shall be changed" (1 Corinthians 15:22). Though the body of the believer has decayed in the ground, his spirit is still alive and is the pledge of resurrection life. We read: "But if the Spirit of Him that raised up Jesus from the dead dwell in you, He that raised up Christ from the dead shall also quicken your mortal bodies by His Spirit that dwelleth in you" (Romans 8:11). If the Holy Spirit, who is the Spirit of Life, is dwelling in you, by that same Spirit will our mortal bodies be quickened into newness of life. This is the victory that Christ wrought for us by His Death and Resurrection. He took hold of death and, grappling with it, compelled it to let go while He ascended triumphantly to glory. And now, unhindered by death, all who are His are permitted to follow after Him into glory also. Abraham Kuyper has said that the redeemed of the Lord truly die, but without ever for one moment coming under the power of death. Giving up the ghost, breathing out the last breath, is for them nothing but passing through the gate, which from this world leads to the world which is with God; and thus for him who dies in Jesus, it is nothing but a passage into eternal life.

One day the Apostle Paul uttered a self-despairing cry, "O wretched man that I am! Who shall deliver me from the body of this death?" The body, yet unredeemed and under the law of sin and death, is a "body of death." But Paul continues: "I thank God (there is deliverance) through Jesus Christ our Lord" (Romans 7:24, 25). Death may seem to triumph for a season as it enters into our homes, and, one by one, takes those nearest and dearest to us. But death cannot be triumphant over the believer in Christ, "for this corruptible must put on incorruption, and this mortal must put on immortality. So when this corruptible shall have put on incorruption, and this mortal shall have put on immortality, then shall be brought to pass the saying that is written, Death is swallowed up in victory" (1 Corinthians 15:53, 54). The child of God has lost all fear of death, and he can look into a grave unafraid. One day I stood by the grave of my godly grandmother and lifted my heart in praise and gratitude to God that death and the grave were conquered by the risen Saviour. I am looking for the return of Christ

and that glad day when the graves shall be opened and the dead
in Christ shall rise first, and together we shall sing: "O death,
where is thy sting? O grave, where is thy victory?"

"Thanks be to God, which giveth us the victory through
our Lord Jesus Christ" (1 Corinthians 15:55, 57).

New Bodies For Old!

The subject of immortality is not of human origin. The
Biblical conception of immortality commences with man being
in right relation to God, and such relationship he cannot attain
by human effort. Man must acknowledge the immortal Christ
as his only hope for life after death. Without the Cross of
Christ there could have been no redemption for the fallen
race, and without that redemption there can be no hope for
the life that is immortal. The Christian possesses a living hope
that finds its root in the Person and Work of the now living
Christ. The Apostle Peter affirms: "Blessed be the God and
Father of our Lord Jesus Christ, which according to His
abundant mercy hath begotten us again unto a lively (or a
living) hope by the resurrection of Jesus Christ from the
dead" (1 Peter 1:3). Though eternal life and immortality are
not synonymous terms, still there can be no immortality of
the body where the spirit of man has not received eternal life
through personal faith in the Lord Jesus Christ. Our Lord could
say to His disciples: "Because I live, ye shall live also" (John
14:19). The resurrection of believers is guaranteed by Christ's
own resurrection.

The Apostle Paul, who, apart from our Lord, was doubtless
the greatest preacher of all time, repeatedly held before Christians this glorious truth. His messages were all Christocentric
and they directed his hearers heavenward "from whence also we
look for the Saviour, the Lord Jesus Christ: Who shall change
our vile body, that it may be fashioned like unto His
glorious body, according to the working whereby He is able
even to subdue all things unto Himself" (Philippians 3:20,
21). This all-glorious fact is the conquering hope of the

Church. William Jennings Bryan has given us a beautiful paragraph on the subject—

> If the Father deigns to touch with divine power the cold and pulseless heart of the buried acorn, and make it burst forth from its prison walls, will He leave neglected in the earth the man, who was made in the image of his Creator? If He stoops to give to the rosebush, whose leaves and withered blossoms float upon the breeze, the sweet assurance of another springtime, will He withhold the words of hope from the souls of men when the frosts of death's winter come? If matter, mute and inanimate, though changed by the forces of nature into a multitude of forms, can never die, will the imperial spirit of man suffer annihilation after it has paid a brief visit, like a royal guest, to this tenement of clay? Rather let us believe that He who in His apparent prodigality wastes not the raindrop, the blade of grass or the evening's zephyr, but makes them all carry out His eternal plans, has given immortality to the mortal, and gathered to Himself the generous spirit of our friends."

In the hour of death and separation from our loved ones we have this comforting belief that the grave is but the gateway to glory. May God grant that you, dear reader, shall receive eternal life and a victorious faith in a life after death.

CHAPTER FOUR

The Consciousness of the Soul After Death

Man Is Created to Endless Existence

Every human being enters the world possessed with *endless existence*. It is true that at death the soul is separated from the body. It is not consistent with the teaching of the Bible to say that at death the soul lapses into a state of complete unconsciousness or even into a deep sleep. The few texts that mendacious scholars have dislodged from their context in order to prove that physical death is the cessation of all consciousness can be easily and understandingly explained when interpreted in the light of the many other passages on this subject.

In Ecclesiastes we read: "The dead know not anything" (Ecclesiastes 9:5). Certainly we all agree that a dead and deteriorating body has absolutely no consciousness of anything past, present, or future. But those who teach "soul-sleep" will find it quite difficult to harmonize their views with other statements that are made by the same writer of Ecclesiastes—

"Then shall the dust return to the earth as it was: and the spirit shall return unto God Who gave it" (Ecclesiastes 12:7). Now we know that this verse is speaking of the body, for in the next verse we read:

"Who knoweth the spirit of man that goeth upward?" (Ecclesiastes 3:21).

Only Man's Body Dies (or Sleeps)

In Scripture we read that man sleeps, but the sleep always is identified with the body. Never once does the Bible refer to the soul sleeping. Where some fall into danger is in identifying man merely with his body and in ignoring the fact that he is a triune being. Man is a trinity; body, soul and spirit. Now the body is not the whole man. Therefore it cannot be concluded that the death of the body is the death of the whole man.

The New Testament Teaches Man's Endless Conscious Existence

The citation of a few New Testament verses makes it clear that man's conscious existence is endless.

"And the graves were opened; and many *bodies* of the saints which slept arose" (Matthew 27:52).

Please notice how the Holy Spirit says that the "bodies" slept. Jesus said:

"Our friend Lazarus *sleepeth;* but I go, that I may awake him out of sleep...Then said Jesus unto them plainly, Lazarus is *dead*" (John 11:11, 14).

Death to our Lord was never anything more than sleep. It is a figure of speech that the Bible applies, for there is never a pause in our consciousness.

Since the soul of man never dies, and the soul is as much a part of man as is his body, then we may say that the dead are alive. The writer became convinced that there was never a pause in man's consciousness while thinking upon the last words of dying men. Think for a moment of our Lord's last words as He hung dying upon the Cross. He said: "Father, into Thy hands I commend my spirit: and having said thus, He gave up the Ghost" (Luke 23:46).

Here Christ is teaching the world the survival of the spiritual part of man after his physical body has died. Death to Jesus was but a passage into the presence of God, not a cold unconscious condition. He knew all about life after death, and He left us with divine assurance that only the body dies. The spirit continues to exist in a conscious state.

Another of our Lord's last words from the Cross proves that death touches only the physical part of man. Let us give consideration to the malefactor hanging on the cross next to the Lord Jesus. This man had not joined the jeering mob, but instead he acknowledged Christ in the face of the Roman opposition. With a contrite spirit and simple faith he said: "Jesus, Lord, remember me when Thou comest into Thy kingdom" (Luke 23:42). The world shall never forget the words which Jesus answered the dying thief. With the soul of this criminal at the very portals of Hell, the dying Saviour said to the dying sinner: "Today shalt thou be with me in Paradise." They were killing his body to be sure, but Jesus promised him that there would be no time of waiting, no pause of sleep or unconsciousness of the soul. Jesus assured him that before that very day had come to a close, he would still be alive and with Christ in Paradise. These words of Christ from the Cross manifest the supreme confidence that He had in a place of blissful life immediately after the believer takes his departure from this earth. If we are called away from this earth today, then "today"—not at some distant period—but immediately, on that very day we shall ascend into His presence. The death of the body is the gateway into a fuller and larger life into which the soul passes.

The martyrdom of Stephen is a strong argument in favor of

the supremacy and the survival of the spiritual part of man. When they stoned Stephen to death, we read that "he fell asleep." This could have no reference whatever to the soul, for it was his body they had pummeled with rocks. As Stephen's body went to its death, earth was receding but Heaven's gate approaching. He knew that he was entering into another sphere of the living. He prayed: "Lord Jesus, receive my spirit" (Acts 7:59). This disciple of Christ did not seek to postpone death or to fight it off. His murderers held no fear for him. He remembered the words of Jesus: "Be not afraid of them that kill the body, and after that have no more that they can do" (Luke 12:4). It is the assurance of immortality and eternal life that enables the servants of Jesus Christ to bear suffering, face all opposition, and die if they are called upon to do so. The scoffing and the scorning of the enemies of Christ can never cheat us out of the presence of our Lord and the place that He has prepared for us.

The Apostle Paul gives us a glimpse into his inner life in an experience that appears only once in all of his writings.

"It is not expedient for me doubtless to glory. I will come to visions and revelations of the Lord. I knew a man in Christ above fourteen years ago, (whether in the body, I cannot tell; or whether out of the body, I cannot tell: God knoweth;) such an one caught up to the third heaven. And I knew such a man, (whether in the body, or out of the body, I cannot tell; God knoweth;) How that he was caught up into paradise, and heard unspeakable words, which it is not lawful for a man to utter" (2 Corinthians 12:1-4).

In this singular but rich experience of Paul's there is valuable material that bears upon our subject. So personal and sacred was this experience that Paul is reticent to tell. There is no doubt that the mighty Apostle is referring to himself although he refers to himself in the third person. Fourteen years before the writing of this Epistle, Paul says that he was caught up into the "third heaven," also called "paradise." The Bible speaks of three heavens. There is the atmospheric heaven in which the birds fly, the heaven where the stars shine, and the third heaven, called paradise, where God is and where His glory is set forth. It was into the third heaven, into the presence of God, where the great apostle was taken. If we study the chronology of Paul's journeys and labors we find that a little more than fourteen years before he wrote his Epistle to the Corinthians he was laboring at Lystra (Acts 14:19). There the Jews stoned him and dragged him outside the city supposing he had been dead. It is generally believed that his experience in paradise to which he refers took place at Lystra while he lay unconscious. He tells us that he was so enraptured by the glories that he saw in Heaven that he did not know whether or not he was there in body—"whether in the body, I cannot tell; or whether out of the body, I cannot tell: God knoweth." Do not overlook the teaching here. It is possible to be fully conscious and yet be absent from the body. Such clear and unmistakable teaching as this of the Apostle Paul defies and defeats the theory of "soul-sleep."

There are three accounts of our Lord's raising the dead. Each time He approached the dead and spoke to him as if he were alive. To the son of the widow of Nain He said: "Young man, I say unto thee, Arise" (Luke 7:14). When Christ came to the daughter of Jairus, we are told: "He took her by the hand, and called, saying, Maid, arise" (Luke 8:54). Finally, He said to the brother of Mary and Martha: "Lazarus, come forth" (John 11:43). In each case Jesus speaks to the person as if he were alive. The soul of man will never enter into a state of non-existence nor unconsciousness.

In Christ's account of the rich man and Lazarus we have the matter summed up and settled that the soul is conscious after death. Both men died and were buried. Though their bodies were in the graves, each of them was alive and conscious. The rich man in Hell could see, hear, speak and feel (Luke 16:19-31).

Let the unsaved heed God's warning. There is a life after death. The unsaved and the saved will be separated from each other. The lost will doubtless carry with them some memories of the past, and their retribution for rejecting Christ will be endless.

But let the believer take courage and be comforted. When we move out of this tabernacle, the real man will leave the body and enter into the presence of the Lord.

CHAPTER FIVE

The Two Resurrections

The resurrection of the human body from the grave is clearly taught in God's Word. Job, the oldest of the patriarchs, said: "For I know that my Redeemer liveth, and that He shall stand at the latter day upon the earth: And though after my skin worms destroy this body, yet in my flesh shall I see God" (Job 19:25, 26). It is evident that Job was firm in his belief in the resurrection of his body and a future life beyond the grave.

Abraham, the founder and father of his race, lived to be one hundred seventy-five years old, and "died in a good old age" (Genesis 25:7, 8), but "he looked for a city which hath foundations, whose builder and maker is God" (Hebrews 11:10). He never saw that city in his earthly pilgrimage, for earth to him was a "strange country." The godly old patriarch shared with others who "desire a better country, that is, an heavenly: wherefore God is not ashamed to be called their God: for He hath prepared for them a city" (Hebrews 11:16). But Abraham believed that the heavenly city would be inhabited by a fleshly body, "accounting that God was able to raise him up, even from the dead..." (Hebrews 11:19).

David was confident of a future life. He said: "My flesh also shall rest in hope" (Psalm 16:9), and "I shall be satisfied, when I awake, with Thy likeness" (Psalm 17:15). These words of the man of God refute the erroneous teaching that the resurrection refers to the spirit of man, and not to his body.

Neither the soul nor the spirit of man dies, but it is his body which dies and is buried. Therefore it must be the body that is raised from the dead, and not the soul or spirit.

When our Lord Jesus was here upon earth, He taught that all men who die will be raised again at some future date. "Marvel not at this: for the hour is coming, in the which *all* that are in the graves shall hear His voice, And shall come forth..." (John 5:28, 29). We affirm and avow our belief in the resurrection of the human body from death and the grave. Without this hope our Christian faith is vain, our brightest hopes are merely bursting bubbles, the Bible is not a true and reliable record, the men who wrote it were poor deluded victims of falsehood, and Jesus Christ is the world's biggest impostor. But so clear is the Bible on the subject of the resurrection that we admit no confusion or doubt.

A Wrong Conception

Many people, among them some Christians, have been taught to believe that there is only one "general" resurrection of all the dead at the end of the world. It is true that all the dead will be raised and brought into judgment, but neither the time, the place, nor the judgments are the same. The Bible clearly distinguishes between a first and a second resurrection.

"...All that are in the graves shall hear His voice, and shall come forth; they that have done good, unto the resurrection of life; and they that have done evil, unto the resurrection of damnation" (John 5:28, 29).

When men are raised, not all will be raised at the same time nor in the same condition. There will be two resurrections for two classes of men. One will be raised to eternal life and immortality, while the other will be raised to condemnation and banishment from the presence of the Lord. There is a "resurrection of life" and a "resurrection of damnation."

"And thou shalt be blessed; for they cannot recompense thee: for thou shalt be recompensed at *the resurrection of the just*" (Luke 14:14).

There is, then, a "resurrection of the just," and since "all shall come forth," there must of necessity be a resurrection of the unjust. Since the dead in Christ shall rise *first,* the implication is that the dead out of Christ (or without Christ) will be raised *afterwards.* When Paul testified before Felix, he said, "that there shall be a resurrection of the dead, both of the just and unjust" (Acts 24:15). The Apostle John makes a clear distinction between the two. He speaks of the redeemed who "lived and reigned with Christ a thousand years. But the rest of the dead lived not again until the thousand years were finished. This is the first resurrection" (Revelation 20:4, 5).

Every believer has passed out of death into life (John 5:24). His life "is hid with Christ in God" (Colossians 3:3), and the exceeding greatness of God's power in resurrection toward us who believe is the same "mighty power which He wrought in Christ, when He raised Him from the dead" (Ephesians 1:19, 20). And by that same power will all the unbelieving dead be brought out of their graves to stand before the judgment of the Great White Throne.

The First Resurrection

"For the Lord Himself shall descend from heaven with a shout, and the voice of the archangel, and with the trump of God; and *the dead in Christ shall rise first*" (1 Thessalonians 4:16).

Surely language could be no clearer than this—"The dead in Christ shall rise first." The time of the First Resurrection is the coming again of our Lord Jesus Christ in the clouds of Heaven to rapture all of the saints to Himself.

At the consummation of the First Resurrection there are three companies of believers who will have been raised at different times. Let us say, for clarity, there are three stages of the resurrection of believers—

(1) When our Lord was crucified on the Cross, we read: "And the graves were opened; and many bodies of the saints which slept arose" (Matthew 27:51, 52).

(2) There is the second stage of the First Resurrection to

which we already have made mention (1 Thessalonians 4:16), when true believers are raised at Christ's first appearance.

(3) The third and final stage of the First Resurrection occurs about seven years later for the multitude of believers who were led to the truth through the witness of the 144,000 during the Tribulation. These are brought forth from the dead just before Christ comes to earth to reign for one thousand years.

Christ the Firstfruits
(I Corinthians 15:20-23).

In the ceremony of the Israelites there were certain national feasts kept annually. The third in order of these was the *Feast of Firstfruits*, an annual occasion of consecration that was solemnized at the beginning of harvest time.

Dr. Martin DeHaan points out that the harvest was divided into three parts. It was one harvest, the fruit of one season, presented on three different occasions. First, there was the sheaf of firstfruits, the earnest or pledge of the greater harvest that would follow. This beautifully typifies the Resurrection of Christ who, by coming forth from the tomb, accomplished the work of the redemption and guaranteed for all who believe in Him a greater resurrection when He returns. "But now is Christ risen from the dead, and become the *firstfruits* of them that slept" (1 Corinthians 15:20). Just as the firstfruits were a pledge of the coming harvest that would be presented to Jehovah, so our Lord's Resurrection is a promise that all who are in their graves who have died trusting Him will be raised and brought into the presence of the Father. Speaking to believers, the Apostle Paul, by the Holy Spirit, says: "For as in Adam all die, even so in Christ shall all be made alive."

After the firstfruits followed the harvesting of the larger part of the crops. We read: "Christ the firstfruits; afterward they that are Christ's at His coming" (1 Corinthians 15:23). Our risen Lord is now in Heaven. Even so, "Our conversation is in Heaven; from whence also we look for the Saviour, the Lord Jesus Christ: who shall change our vile body, that it may be fashioned like unto His glorious body, according to the working whereby He is able even to subdue all things unto Himself" (Philippians 3:20, 21). He will come again even as He said. Christ the firstfruits; afterward they that are Christ's at His coming.

But the harvest is not ended as yet. It is not completed until the gleanings are added. Always there are loose ears that fall by the way, and these must be gathered up. The gleanings are those tribulation saints who had not heard and believed the Gospel before the rapture of the Church. So we have Christ the firstfruits, then we have the harvest or the resurrection of the saved at the rapture, and finally the gleanings or the saved of the seven year's tribulation period. Then follows the millennial age during which all the saints of every age will reign with Christ a thousand years. What bright prospect for those who put their trust in the Son of God! But tell me, are you prepared for the coming of the Lord and the First Resurrection?

The Second Resurrection

When the thousand years are expired, Satan will be loosed for a season and will carry on his rebellion where he left off before the millennium when he was cast into the bottomless pit. Then God will have done with Satan forever, for "the devil that deceived them was cast into the lake of fire and brimstone, where the beast and the false prophet are, and shall be tormented day and night forever and ever" (Revelation 20:10). We shudder at this unceasing torment without intermission, this never-ending existence in painful agony.

But the devil's doom is not the blackest page in the Biblical records of God's dealings. There is yet an account to be settled with all those who died in rejection of the Lord Jesus Christ. A Great White Throne has been erected. We are about to view the greatest assize ever conducted. The Judge is our Lord Jesus Himself, for "The Father judgeth no man, but hath committed all judgment unto the Son" (John 5:22). This is the resurrection of the unbelieving dead, who remained "dead in trespasses and sins" (Ephesians 2:1). Though they are spiritually dead having not eternal life, they are standing before God physically alive in their resurrection bodies, to receive the final sentence, banishment from the presence of God and eternal punishment in the lake of fire.

Many unbelievers seek to stifle their conscience by uttering their unbelief in a physical resurrection. They count it a thing incredible that God could raise a physical body that had been trampled under the dust for more than one thousand years.

The Resurrection of Jesus Christ is the confirmation of the resurrection of the human body and future judgment. When the mighty Apostle Paul preached his sermon to the Athenians on Mars' hill, he said that God commands all men everywhere to repent, "because He hath appointed a day, in the which He will judge the world in righteousness by that Man whom He hath ordained; whereof He hath given assurance unto all men, in that He hath raised Him from the dead" (Acts 17:31). Since both Judge and day of judgment already have been appointed, man must be raised after death if the purposes of God are to be fulfilled. Certainly they are not dead men whom God will arraign before his solemn tribunal. They will be alive and conscious of that great hour. So in order that man might be assured of a future judgment, Christ arose as the criterion of the law of resurrection. The living Christ is a positive attestation of the fact that there is a day of judgment.

The last judgment in the Bible will be that of the unsaved dead who will stand before the Great White Throne in living, resurrected bodies to receive their final sentence of doom and be cast into the lake of fire. This will not be a judgment to see if sinners are lost, for they are lost already because "he that believeth not is condemned already" (John 3:18). Christians will be present, but only as witnesses. The judged will be those of the Second Resurrection whose bodies have been brought out of the grave and whose spirits brought back from Hell.

All of the unsaved, "small and great, stand before God" (Revelation 20:12). In our human courts of law it is often the case that the defendant does not appear. Sometimes a witness, a juror, or a judge can be bribed, and the guilty one escapes trial and the passing of sentence. Sometimes false witnesses can turn court's evidence and the guilty one goes free. But in that day, the books are opened, including the Book of Life, "and the dead were judged out of those things which were written in the books according to their works" (Revelation 20:12). While it is true that millions have lived and died of whom the world knows nothing, their thoughts and deeds are divinely written where the memory of them can never perish. An accurately guided hand has recorded the biography of all, and all evil will be accounted for in that dreadfully solemn hour. If you have despised Jesus here, it will mean judgment there. If you have belittled the invitation to Heaven while here, you will be cast into Hell then.

A Literal, Physical Body

Only a part of the human race has agreed with the testimony of God the Father which He has given concerning His Son. But at the final judgment, every unbeliever of every age will bow the knee that once he refused to bend, and confess with the tongue that once he refused to confess Christ with. Yes, literal knees and tongues of every Christ-rejecting sinner will bow and confess in utter humility the Christ they spurned and scoffed at here on earth.

Again we repeat that God finds no pleasure in the death of the wicked. He would rather save than have them die in unbelief, but whosoever is not found written in the Book of Life will be cast into the lake of fire. They shall have their part in the lake which burns with fire and brimstone. This is the second death (Revelation 20:15; 21:8). If you die in your sins, the judgment is sure and certain. You will not escape! No, you cannot escape. If, while you read this message, you realize your need of Christ as your personal Saviour from sin, confess that you are a sinner and trust Christ to save you. "Blessed and holy is he that hath part in the first resurrection" (Revelation 20:6).

CHAPTER SIX

The Resurrection Body

"With what body do they come?" (1 Corinthians 15:35).

Death—The Sleep of the Body

No Biblical description of death is so comforting and consoling to the believer as that which is revealed in the familiar word *sleep*. It is a word that applies to the body only and never to the soul. Our Lord said to His disciples: "Our friend Lazarus *sleepeth;* but I go that I may awake him out of sleep. Then said His disciples, Lord, if he sleep, he shall do well. Howbeit Jesus spake of his death" (John 11:11-13). Of the martyrdom and death of Stephen, we read: "He fell *asleep*" (Acts 7:60). When the Apostle Paul was yet alive, he said that of the five hundred brethren who had seen Christ alive after His Resurrection, "some are fallen *asleep*" (1 Corinthians 15:6). His comforting message to the believers at Thessalonica was, "I would not have you to be ignorant, brethren, concerning them which are *asleep*" (1 Thessalonians 4:13). The Apostle Peter, speaking of Old Testament saints, said: "The fathers fell *asleep*" (2 Peter 3:4).

The Old Testament saints were comforted by this same truth. More than forty times in the Old Testament it is said of a man who died that he "slept with his fathers." "And the LORD said unto Moses, Behold, thou shalt sleep with thy fathers" (Deuteronomy 31:16; 2 Samuel 7:12). Job said: "Now shall I sleep in the dust; and thou shalt seek me in the morning, but I shall not be" (Job 7:21). In these verses we have a transcendently sublime description of death which assures the believer that it is but "the transient slumber of the body, to be followed by the glorious awakening at the sound of the last trumpet."

Death—A Temporary Separation of the Spiritual From the Physical

This temporary suspension of the activities of the body does not mean that the spirit of man is asleep. The body is but the tabernacle or dwelling place of the spirit part of man. Upon the death of the body, the spirit of a believer takes departure, closing the senses of the body until the day of its resurrection. Immediately upon the death of our bodies, we leave the flesh, "to depart, and to be with Christ" (Philippians 1:23), "waiting for the adoption, to wit, the redemption of our body" (Romans 8:23).

Raised To Be Like Jesus

Death is not to be feared by the Christian. We shall live in a literal body just as real as the one we have now, for, says Paul: "We look for the Saviour, the Lord Jesus Christ: Who shall change our vile body, that it may be fashioned like unto His glorious body...." (Philippians 3:20, 21). The coming of our Lord in the air to take us to Heaven will necessitate a change in this purchased body of corruption. The body is as much the Lord's purchased possession as is the soul. It is dear to Him. "The body is...for the Lord; and the Lord for the body" (1 Corinthians 6:13). The goal of the Gospel is to bring eternal life and immortality to all who will believe. Since the body of the saints will be "fashioned like unto His glorious body," we may well wonder what our bodies will be like at the resurrection. John says: "We know that, when He shall appear, we shall be like Him; for we shall see Him as He is" (1 John 3:2). When our Lord ascended into Heaven, He was thirty-three years of age, a young man in the strength and glory of His youth. Senility had not overtaken our Lord when He died upon the Cross for our sins. In David's Psalm of the exalted Christ in the glory, we read: "Thou hast the dew of Thy youth" (Psalm 110:3). O wondrous thought! We shall be clothed upon with perennial youth. We shall be like Him, fashioned like unto His glorious body.

Christ shall "*change* our vile body" (Philippians 3:21) we read. The word "change" means to *transfigure*. It has been suggested that we have here the thought of metamorphosis which is a remarkable change in the form and structure of a living body. When our Lord took Peter, James, and John up into the Holy Mountain, we read that "He was *transfigured* before them" (Matthew 17:2). Christ appeared during that brief period of time in His glorified body. He was transfigured (or metamorphosed) before them. It was a body like His post-resurrection body when He appeared to His disciples behind shut doors (John 20:19). The change of the believer at the resurrection has to do with his body, wherein resides the sin principle, for even the Christian must admit, "I know that in me (that is in my flesh), there dwelleth no good thing" (Romans 7:18). The word "change" could not refer to the spiritual part of man, for, as Kenneth Wuest says: "The word 'change' is the translation of a Greek word which speaks of an expression which is assumed from the outside, which act brings about a change of outward expression."

Biologically speaking, the change of a caterpillar into a butterfly is spoken of as a "metamorphosis." The ugly, repulsive caterpillar is confined to a tomb which it spins for itself. While in the cocoon there is an apparently dead and formless substance. But after the warm sun of spring has beaten its golden rays upon that cocoon, there comes forth a beautiful butterfly. Though the butterfly is different in appearance from the caterpillar, we recognize the beautiful winged insect as being the same as the caterpillar. It is the same living creature, yet different. So also is the resurrection of the body. Now we have a vile body (or a body of humiliation). The Apostle James calls it a "low" body, "because as the flower of the grass he shall pass away" (James 1:10). The body of Adam, in its original state, was provided with a covering of glory, but when sin entered, the covering of glory was replaced with a covering of humiliation. In our present bodies of humiliation we are unfit for the glories of Heaven and God's presence, but hopefully we look for our Lord's return when He shall fashion our bodies of humiliation like unto His own body of glory. It will be the same body in that it will be recognizable, but wonderfully changed.

Answering The Skeptic

Some unbelieving skeptics have proposed the argument that it will be impossible for the same body to be raised since the bodies of those who have been dead for hundreds of years have become decomposed into integrant parts; that is, reduced to powder.

God anticipated this problem. We read: "But some man will say, How are the dead raised up? and with what body do they come" (1 Corinthians 15:35)? To answer this, the Apostle, by the Holy Spirit, uses the illustration of a farmer sowing grain. When a farmer drops a kernel of grain into the ground, he knows that when the seed dies or seemingly rots away, that does not mean the end of his efforts. He knows that the one seed will come forth into a fuller life, producing a stalk with several ears bearing many hundreds of kernels like the one he planted. The actual seed that was planted he does not see. Yet there is absolute identity. It is the same with the resurrection of our bodies. "That which thou sowest is not quickened, except it die: And that which thou sowest, thou sowest not that body that shall be, but bare grain, it may chance of wheat, or of some other grain: But God giveth it a body as it hath pleased Him, and to every seed his own body" (1 Corinthians 15:35-38).

It will not be necessary for God to use every part of this body when he raises it from the grave. Such a thought is not taught in Scripture. In fact, it is scientifically true that the component parts of our bodies undergo periodical changes. We are told that through the change of elements, we receive new bodies every seven years. We may not be conscious of the change. Nevertheless we have not the same body today that we had seven years ago. There is an identity that we maintain all of our lifetime, and yet there is not one cell in our bodies that was there seven years ago. In the resurrection the bodies of the saints will bear their individual identities. Dr. Wilbur M. Smith has said: "The fact that after death our physical substance disintegrates and scatters, creates no difficulties for God, so that He could not bring those bodies back gloriously transformed." By the new birth we are born again into the Kingdom of God, a Kingdom that can never break down or disintegrate. Because sin can never enter, there is no danger of corruptibility. The resurrection will be the occasion when our bodies become incorruptible and will inherit the Kingdom of God.

From Corruption to Incorruption
From Mortality to Immortality

"It is sown in corruption; it is raised in incorruption" (1 Corinthians 15:42).

"For this corruptible must put on incorruption" (1 Corinthians 15:53).

Death is written on the face of all that is alive. The moment we begin to live we commence to die. But if we are to have bodies in Heaven, we must have bodies that are free from corruption. This is exactly the kind of body that Christ will give us when He comes. It was buried in corruption, but it will be raised in incorruption. We have some idea of an incorruptible body in the scene on the Mount of Transfiguration. Moses and Elijah both appeared with Christ. Moses had died fifteen hundred years before. Yet he was there recognizable in a glorious body. Elijah had been caught up to Heaven without dying about nine hundred years before, and he too was there in a glorified body.

From Dishonor To Glory

"It is sown in dishonor; it is raised in glory" (1 Corinthians 15:43).

The body that is put in the grave is sown in dishonor. The average Christian sadly neglects his body, failing to realize that it is the temple of the Holy Spirit. Proper care of the body is far more the exception than it is the rule. The bodies of some Christians have been broken and diseased by sin before the persons ever came to a knowledge of the truth. But our resurrection bodies will be raised in glory. We shall be like Jesus, in the brightness of His glory. O glorious hope!

From Weakness to Power

"It is sown in weakness; it is raised in power" (1 Corinthians 15:43).

It is believed that the Apostle Paul was frail in body, afflicted with "a thorn in the flesh." Weak bodies have their limitations, and many of us can testify as to how the work of the Lord often is hampered by bodily limitations. The tasks we seek to perform become wearisome by reason of the infirmities of the flesh. But in Heaven we shall know nothing of physical weakness. The limitations of earth are not known in Heaven. What a glorious change that will be! Raised in power!

From the Natural To the Spiritual

"It is sown a natural body; it is raised a spiritual body" (1 Corinthians 15:44).

It must be clearly understood that the phrase "a spiritual body" does not so much as infer that the resurrection body will be a body without substance. The word "natural" is from a word used by the Greeks when they spoke of the soul of man. We pointed out earlier in this volume how that man was made of three component parts: body, soul, and spirit. In the physical he possesses world-consciousness through his five senses. With his soul, which is the seat of his emotions, he possesses self-consciousness, thereby having knowledge that he is a personality. By his spirit, he is enabled to know God and to worship and serve Him after his human spirit has been quickened by the Holy Spirit. Our bodies while on earth are natural or soulish bodies and are engaged chiefly with the activities and the environment of earth. By nature it becomes easily adjusted to work and play. The spiritual life is not absent altogether from man, but it occupies a small part of his time and energy as compared with his soul life.

When the resurrection body is called "a spiritual body," it is not meant that it will be composed of intangible substance. Robert S. Candlish has said: "The words natural and spiritual, as applied to the body, have respect not so much to the nature of the substance of which the body is composed, as to the uses or purposes which it is intended to serve." On earth we are occupied to a greater degree with the natural body, while in Heaven in our resurrection bodies we will be occupied with all that pertains to God and godliness. The spiritual life of man will prevail.

We might say that the body has two masters, a natural and a spiritual. Paul said: "When I would do good, evil is present with me" (Romans 7:21). The Apostle was truly God's child by the transforming power of the Holy Spirit, but the natural man was still very much alive and warring against the spiritual. And each of us knows too well what a barrier the natural man is! We are hindered by the attitude of the natural toward the spiritual. But in Heaven we shall be clothed with a resurrection body where the higher principles in man will predominate and the full tide of spiritual life will be in control.

In Heaven all will be incorrupt, immortal, glorious, powerful, and spiritual. Before the throne of God we will serve Him eternally in His temple. O glorious hope! O resurrection day!

CHAPTER SEVEN

The Future Judgment of the Believer

Believers never need fear a condemnatory judgment for sin. For every Christian this judgment is already past. When Jesus comes again He will have in His body the marks of crucifixion, and this will prove that the penalty for sin has been paid in full. Our Lord reassures us by His own word: "Verily, verily, I say unto you, He that heareth My word, and believeth on Him that sent Me, hath everlasting life, *and shall not come into condemnation;* but is passed from death unto life" (John 5:24). To this the Apostle Paul adds: "There is therefore now no condemnation to them which are in Christ Jesus" (Romans 8:1). Our souls rest forever upon these eternal words of our God.

All Men And Fallen Angels Are To Be Judged

Yet the Bible teaches clearly that all men, both living and dead, saved and unsaved, must give an account to Christ. The Apostle Peter, in his great sermon in the house of Cornelius, said "that it is He which was ordained of God to be the Judge of quick and dead" (Acts 10:42). Later, in his First Epistle, Peter wrote that the saints "shall give account to Him that is ready to judge the quick (the living) and the dead" (1 Peter 4:5). Those who were dead, those who have died since or will have died, and the living must give account to Jesus Christ who is ready to judge all men.

The Five Separate Future Judgments

Not all men will be judged at the same time and place. There are five future judgments. The first of these will be the judgment of the believer's works, called "The Judgment Seat of Christ." It is this judgment to which we shall give consideration in this chapter. But first, we shall outline the four future judgments that will follow the judgment of the believer's works.

The Judgment of Regathered Israel. In Daniel 12:1 this judgment is called "The Time of Jacob's Trouble." It will be the punishment of the Jews for their disobedience to God and their rejection of Jesus Christ. During the Tribulation Period and after the close of the present Age of Grace, Israel will pay for her sins, being afflicted with unprecedented misery.

The Judgment of the Living Nations. At the end of the Tribulation Period, after Israel has been judged, the nations of the earth will be judged by Christ and His Church. This judgment will not be against individuals but against nations for their treatment of the Jewish people.

The Judgment of Fallen Angels. This is the final judgment against Satan and other fallen angels who will be judged with him. Immediately after the one thousand years of the Kingdom Age, Satan and his hosts will meet their doom. At that time we shall see the final fulfillment of that great prophecy in Genesis 3:15.

The Judgment of the Unbelieving Dead. This is called the Great White Throne Judgment. After the casting of Satan into Hell, the wicked dead will be raised to receive the final sentence of condemnation (Revelation 20:12-15). No believer will be judged at that day as the final judgment is reserved for all who rejected the Lord Jesus Christ on earth.

The Judgment Seat Of Christ

The first future judgment derives its name from two passages where the term "Judgment Seat of Christ" appears—

"For we shall all stand before the judgment seat of Christ" (Romans 14:10).

"For we must all appear before the judgment seat of Christ" (2 Corinthians 5:10).

This judgment cannot be confused with either of the other judgments because the Holy Spirit used a Greek word to describe the Judgment Seat of Christ that is peculiar and different from the Greek words used in connection with other judgments. Here the word used is *bema*. It appears in classical Greek to identify the seat in the arena of the Olympic games whereon the judge sat, not to punish contestants, but to present awards to the victors. When Christians stand before the *bema* of Christ, it will be for the express purpose of being rewarded according to their works. There is no idea of punishment.

1. *The Judge.* Our Lord Himself said: "The Father judgeth no man, but hath committed all judgment unto the Son" (John 5:22). In this sense every judgment throne can be considered as the judgment seat of Christ. However, there is only one *bema*, a throne erected for Christ for the purpose of awarding the prizes or crowns to the victorious saints.

Since Christ is the Judge, and a time and place have been set for the judgment of believers, we are warned against any attempt at judging each other in this life. "Why dost thou judge thy brother? or why dost thou set at nought thy brother? for we shall all stand before the judgment seat of Christ" (Romans 14:10). We are not judges. Therefore we have no right to judge or to despise our brother. It is not possible for any of us to judge righteously and justly because we do not know the hearts of each other. Jesus warned His disciples: "Judge not, that ye be not judged (Matthew 7:1). We must exercise a careful discrimination in all matters, but our attitude is to be without censoriousness. We are expected to use our reason and the powers of discernment, but never to avenge, condemn, nor damn another. Abraham Kuyper has said: "All human judgment remains imperfect. It can never fully satisfy our thirst after justice." A human tribunal cannot bring a just retribution upon those who have committed crimes in secret. Too frequently the guilty are set free and the innocent condemned. "Forget not your martyrs." Because of our limitations we come to wrong conclusions. Therefore we are to leave all judgment with the omniscient Judge who will judge righteously and accurately, but never falsely. When Jesus comes, every Christian, dead or alive will be included in the great throng that will stand before the *bema* of Christ. We will be there, not merely as spectators or witnesses. The Holy Judge will not need anyone to witness. In that day His word shall stand. "He knew all men, and needed not that any should testify of man: for He knew what was in man" (John 2:24, 25).

2. *The Judged.* Only believers will appear before the Judgment Seat of Christ. In both verses where this judgment is mentioned (Romans 14:10; 2 Corinthians 5:10), the words are addressed to Christians only. All the wicked dead (unbelievers) will be judged at the Great White Throne after the one thousand years' reign of Christ on earth. But the subjects to whom the Apostle Paul addressed his messages when he said, "We must all appear," were exclusively the saints of whom Paul considered himself one. Someone will question the possibility of standing room for the countless millions of saints, or another may question the time element of such "an endlessly drawn out pronouncement of judgment upon so large a host of individuals." The Bible is silent on details as to the exact location of the place of judgment. Whether in Heaven or in the air we cannot tell. However, one thing is certain, as Henry W.

Frost has said: "A divine judgment need not take long." It is absurd even to conceive of a problem of space when we think of the vast expanse in the heavens. "It is possible that this judgment of the saints will be instantaneous, and that each Christian will rise into the air to enter at once into his proper place and appointed rewarding." If there are problems regarding the exact location and the manner of this judgment, there are none regarding its certainty, "For *we must all appear* before the judgment seat of Christ."

The Christian's Works Will Be Tested

Let us pause to read carefully the Holy Spirit's message concerning Christian work and its rewards—

"For we are labourers together with God: ye are God's husbandry, ye are God's building. According to the grace of God which is given unto me, as a wise masterbuilder, I have laid the foundation, and another buildeth thereon. But let every man take heed how he buildeth thereupon. For other foundation can no man lay than that is laid, which is Jesus Christ. Now if any man build upon this foundation gold, silver, precious stones, wood, hay, stubble; Every man's work shall be made manifest: for the day shall declare it, because it shall be revealed by fire; and the fire shall try every man's work of what sort it is. If any man's work abide which he hath built thereupon, he shall receive a reward. If any man's work shall be burned, he shall suffer loss: but he himself shall be saved; yet so as by fire" (1 Corinthians 3:9-15),

The great Apostle refers to himself and all of his fellow-workers as "laborers together with God." This is a wonderful truth when we realize that God does not actually need any one of us to do His work. It is not necessary that He should consider us at all to carry His Gospel, for He can carry out the whole plan of salvation without us. He could send His holy angels to spread redemption's message, or He could flash it across the skies to the visibility of every person in the universe, but He has chosen the believer to tell the story of His sovereign grace and matchless love.

The foundation for this work is already laid, "For other

foundation can no man lay than that is laid, which is Jesus Christ"(verse 11). Now we are to build upon this foundation, and the work in which we engage ourselves must stand the test of the judgment seat of Christ if we are to receive a reward. "Every man's work shall be made manifest... and the fire shall try every man's work of what sort it is." Many Christians who have labored humbly and prayerfully in the Spirit will be rewarded, but that which was done in the energy of the flesh and which is merely called "Christian work" will be consumed by the fire of purging. "If a man's work abide, he shall receive a reward. If a man's work shall be burned, he shall suffer loss." "*We* shall be judged" according to the secret motives and the character of our work. If you cannot do all that you would like to do, be sure that whatever you do is of the right "sort." This means that if our work is of the right kind or character, we will receive a reward. Contrariwise, if what a believer does is not of the right character, "he shall suffer loss: but he himself shall be saved; yet so as by fire" (1 Corinthians 3:15).

In an interesting and instructive parable of our Lord recorded by Luke (Luke 18:11-27), we have a picture of this present age and the Christian's responsibility. "A certain nobleman went into a far country to receive for himself a kingdom, and to return. And he called his ten servants, and delivered them ten pounds, and said unto them, Occupy till I come." The ten pounds were divided equally among the ten servants, thus showing that each servant had an equal opportunity during the Lord's absence. To each of us has been committed the witness of Jesus Christ. We are to share in the opportunities and responsibilities of making Him known. Not one single Christian can say that he is not responsible for the spreading of the truth of the Gospel. During our Lord's absence we are to occupy till He comes, for He is coming again, as He said, to render to every man according to his deeds.

"When he was returned, having received the kingdom, then he commanded these servants to be called unto him, to whom he had given the money, that he might know how much every man had gained by trading." Here our Lord describes what will happen when He returns. All of us who are His shall be called unto Him to give an account of ourselves as to how we discharged our responsibilities during His absence. This is the Judgment Seat of Christ, and it will determine our position and service in the Millennial Kingdom. Recently in Philadelphia two men took the same examination with the understanding that the one receiving the highest grade would be appointed to the office of Chief of the Fire Bureau. It is by the same method of competitive examination in faithfulness that the saints will be appointed to rule with Christ. In the parable the servant who gained ten pounds was called "faithful," and was given authority over ten cities. Likewise the servant which gained five pounds was given authority over five cities. But the servant who returned his one pound having done nothing with it was sternly rebuked. The Lord said: "Take the pound, and give it to him that hath ten pounds."

When Jesus comes each believer will receive his or her just reward for service according to the measure and motive of our works. No rewards will be given by political preferment, but only in exact proportion to the genuine effort put forth. Other parables of our Lord which should be studied in connection with Christian service are the Unprofitable Servant (Luke 17:7-10), The Laborers in the Vineyard (Matthew 20:1-16), and The Talents (Matthew 25:14-30).

Saints Will Differ In Heaven

The Apostle Paul says: "There is one glory of the sun, and another glory of the moon, and another glory of the stars: for one star differeth from another star in glory. So also is the resurrection of the dead" (1 Corinthians 15:41, 42). All believers will have glorified bodies, but there will be difference in glory according to the measure of our diligence and devotedness to Christ and His work. I hold in my hand three coins. One is gold, one is silver, and the third is copper. All three bear the same inscription of the United States of America. However, the glory of the gold is one glory, the glory of the silver is a lesser glory, and the glory of the copper is yet a lesser glory than either the gold or the silver. So also is the resurrection of the dead. Each of the bodies of the saved will bear the glorified and heavenly mark of distinction, but the glory of some will differ from the glory of others. Our capacity to serve in Heaven we will take with us when Jesus comes.

The Crowns or Rewards

"Behold, I come quickly: hold that fast which thou hast, that no man take thy crown" (Revelation 3:11).

"And, behold, I come quickly; and My reward is with Me, to give every man according as his work shall be" (Revelation 22:12).

The Judgment Seat of Christ will be a crowning day for those Christians who will receive rewards for their works. The New Testament teaches that there are five such "crowns" to be given.

The Incorruptible Crown. "And every man that striveth for the mastery is temperate in all things. Now they do it to obtain a corruptible crown; but we an incorruptible" (1 Corinthians 9:25). Here Paul has in mind the athlete in the Roman arena. Before the contest each participant practiced self-discipline, being temperate in all things. There were doubtless many pleasures and pastimes that the athletes might have entered into and enjoyed, but they denied themselves these things in order to do their best. A crown awaited the victor. The incorruptible crown for the Christian is the victor's crown for those who keep under the body and bring it into subjection. If an athlete must subject himself to many months of rigid discipline and training to obtain a corruptible crown, how much more should we bring our bodies into subjection for a crown that is incorruptible!

The Crown of Rejoicing. "For what is our hope, or joy, or crown of rejoicing? Are not even ye in the presence of our

Lord Jesus Christ at His coming? For ye are our glory and joy" (1 Thessalonians 2:19, 20). This is the soul-winner's crown. The first thing that a Christian should pray for and seek to cultivate is the desire, ability, and wisdom to win lost souls to Jesus Christ. Paul was confident that when he would stand before the Judgment Seat of Christ the Thessalonian converts would guarantee a crown for all those who shared in bringing them to Christ.

The Crown of Righteousness. "Henceforth there is laid up for me a crown of righteousness, which the Lord, the righteous judge, shall give me at that day: and not to me only, but unto them also that love His appearing" (2 Timothy 4:8). Here the character of the reward corresponds to the character of the Giver. Both are said to be righteous. The doctrine of our Lord's return is regarded very highly by God. In spite of the fact that Jesus said He would come again, there are many people who scoff at the thought of Christ's appearing. This and kindred truths have brought suffering and hardship, and in some cases death, to those who insisted on preaching and teaching them. But how wonderful to know that God has prepared a special reward for all who look for that blessed hope, who wait for His Son from Heaven, and who love His appearing!

The Crown of Life. "Blessed is the man that endureth temptation: for when he is tried, he shall receive the crown of life, which the Lord hath promised to them that love Him" (James 1:12).

The Crown of Life is reserved for those who have given their lives for the sake of the Gospel. Not all of our Lord's witnesses have been called to suffering and martyrdom. Not all would willingly pay with their lives to take the message of salvation to the lost. How thoughtful and just our heavenly Father was when He prepared a martyr's crown for those who suffer persecution for Christ's sake!

The Crown of Glory. "Feed the flock of God which is among you, taking the oversight thereof, not by constraint, but willingly; not for filthy lucre, but of a ready mind; Neither as being lords over God's heritage, but being ensamples to the flock. And when the chief Shepherd shall appear, ye shall receive a crown of glory that fadeth not away" (1 Peter 5:2-5). There are many who have been called and ordained by God to preach and teach His Word. These are the under-shepherds who care for the flock of God during the absence of the Chief Shepherd. Let us give ourselves without ostentation to the care of the sheep of His pasture, for the crown of unfading glory awaits us when the Chief Shepherd shall appear.

If there is to be joy and rejoicing for those who receive the crowns, surely there will be disappointment and sorrow for those who will not receive them. Will there be no regret, no shame, no consternation? Listen once again to God's declaration: "If a man's work shall be burned, he shall suffer..."

The Judgment Seat of Christ seems a necessity to the writer. Think of the believers, all members of the body of Christ, who are divided because of differences. Now if our Lord returns before there is a reconciliation of such Christians here on earth, it is necessary that they get right with each other somewhere, for certainly they cannot continue on forever in holding hatred and animosity in their hearts. Heaven knows no such actions. Hatred and unforgiveness is sin. Yet there is no sin Heaven. Hence the necessity of the Judgment Seat.

The Judgment Seat of Christ is necessary because not one believer has received his reward for any service he has rendered in this life. Often, and frequently at funerals, we hear it said that the departed one has gone to his eternal reward. This is not Scripturally correct. The departed saints are with the Lord, but not one has received his reward as yet. We are not rewarded one by one at death. None of the disciples nor the apostles has received his rewards yet, nor will he until Jesus comes back and all saints are gathered together.

One final word! "And now, little children, abide in Him; that, when He shall appear, we may have confidence, and not be ashamed before Him at His coming" (1 John 2:28). Ashamed

at His coming! What a sorry closing chapter for any believer's life! How ashamed we will be if we are engaged in dis-
honest business, unclean conversation, or unholy living! Let
us, with singleness of purpose, abandon ourselves to His perfect
will for our lives so that we may hear His: "Well done."

CHAPTER EIGHT

The Eternal Punishment of the Lost

This chapter is an endeavor to write a statement of the most
solemn doctrine in all the Bible. When I first attempted to
preach on this subject some years ago, invariably I found my-
self asking God for tenderness in presenting it. Today I must
confess that there still lingers an averseness on my part to declare that there is no hope that any measure of divine grace or
mercy ever will be extended to one person after death, but
that there is rather a fearful anticipation of retribution in
the lake of fire.

Hell—An Unpopular Subject

Furthermore, I am aware of the fact that this subject is an
unpopular one. Since those memorable days when Jonathan
Edwards preached that potent and moving sermon on "Sinners
in the Hands of an Angry God," the doctrine of the eternal
retribution of the lost has gradually gone into obscurity.

When Irvin S. Cobb, the internationally famous humorist
and writer, died in March 1944, he referred to Heaven as "a
powerfully dull place, populated to a considerable and uncom-
fortable degree by prigs, time-servers and unpleasantly agres-
sive individuals," and then he added that "hell may have a
worse climate but undoubtedly the company is sprightlier." Of
course Cobb did not believe in Hell, for he insisted that those
in charge of his burial "avoid reading the so-called Christian
burial service, which, in view of the language employed in it,

I regard as one of the most cruel and paganish things inherited by our forbears from our remote pagan ancestry. Instead, let the 23rd Psalm be read. This has no threat of eternal hell fire."

Irvin Cobb was doubtless a success as a humorist, but no amount of jocose treatment of Hell can deliver him from the anguish and agony of his soul today.

False Theories

Many conflicting theories have been formed regarding this subject. Of course, those mentioned under the above heading are human theories that have not the support of the Word of God. Here we can do little more than make a passing reference to these man-made ideas. These are: *Conditional Immortality, Universalism* and the *Restoration Theory.*

Conditional Immortality. This theory is built on the error that all who do not receive everlasting life will die as the animals and be annihilated or wiped out of existence. It contends that immortality is conditional upon receiving the gift of everlasting life. If anyone dies not having the gift of everlasting life he shall not be punished with everlasting torment. He shall be annihilated.

Universalism. The universalistic theory holds the idea of universal redemption. For example, a certain number of Scripture references are used to prove that Christ died for all men alike. Therefore all men alike shall be saved in the end. Universalism uses such texts as Paul's when he said: "We preach, warning every man, and teaching every man in all wisdom; that we may present every man perfect in Christ Jesus" (Colossians 1:28). Certainly the Apostle could not have meant that he expected every man that ever came into the world to be made perfect in Christ. The words "every man" could refer only to those to whom Paul addressed his Epistle; namely, "To the saints and faithful brethren in Christ" (1:2). This theory does not deny that all men are lost by sin, but it contends that all men will finally be saved and enter into everlasting life. Universalism falls when it overlooks the Biblical fact that salvation and everlasting life are applied to no one apart from his personal acceptance of it as a divinely bestowed gift to "whosoever will."

The Restoration Theory. This view, called by some, *Restitutionism,* appeals to the universalist, in that it does not deny that all men are lost, but that sometime, somewhere, all creation (including Satan and the fallen angels) will be restored or reconciled to God. Being contrary to reason and common sense, the average person labels this view as preposterous. But let us look at two texts that are used to form the basis of the false view of Restitutionism. The words of our Lord are quoted: "And I, if I be lifted up from the earth, will draw *all men* unto Me" (John 12:32). We must exercise care that these words of Christ do not lead us to believe the heretical teaching of Restitutionism. Our Saviour never meant that all men finally shall be saved by His crucifixion. Dr. A. C. Gaebelein in his commentary on "The Gospel of John" says: "The analogy of other texts shows plainly that the only reasonable sense is, that Christ's crucifixion would have a 'drawing' influence on men of all nations, Gentiles as well as Jews." But it is quite possible also that this verse has a future application. In the preceding verse (31) which was given in connection with verse thirty-two, Jesus spoke of the future when "the prince of this world shall be cast out." Of a truth, in that day "all men" will be drawn unto Him.

Another favorite text used by the Restitutionists is one of Peter's statements given in his second sermon after Pentecost. The Apostle said:

> "Repent ye therefore, and be converted, that your sins may be blotted out, when the times of refreshing shall come from the presence of the Lord; And he shall send Jesus Christ, which before was preached unto you: Whom the heaven must receive until the times of restitution of all things, which God hath spoken by the mouth of all his holy prophets since the world began" Acts 3:19-21).

Again the teachers of this false doctrine have seized upon a phrase and have deliberately torn it from its context to make it fit their scheme of thought. The phrase "restitution of all things" cannot be interpreted correctly if applied to any other than the house of Israel. Remember, it is to Israel that Peter is addressing his message. His introductory statement was: "Ye men of Israel" (vs. 12). It is the restitution of all things for Israel when Christ comes to restore the nation to which the apostle is referring. Furthermore, it is to be the "restitution of all things, which God hath spoken *by the mouth of all His holy prophets.*" Immediately we are limited in defining Peter's statement, for we must confine it to the restitution (or restoration) of which the prophets spoke. Frequently the prophets wrote of the restoration of Israel to the land of Palestine, but nowhere in the prophetic writings have we ever come across so much as an inference that the wicked dead ever will be saved.

Restitutionism depends largely upon that mighty statement uttered by the Apostle Paul in Philippians 2:10, 11, "That at the name of Jesus every knee should bow, of things in heaven, and things in earth, and things under the earth; and that every tongue should confess that Jesus Christ is Lord, to the glory of God the Father." This passage means that all creation, whether animate or inanimate, in heaven, on earth, or under the earth, will confess (or publicly declare) and thereby agree to the testimony that God the Father has given of His Son. There is not the slightest indication that all men who acknowledge the authority of Christ *must* be saved or that they *will* be saved. While our Lord was here on earth the demons frequently acknowledged His authority (See Mark 1:24, 34; 3:11, 12), and we know that everlasting fire is prepared for the Devil and his angels (Matthew 25:41).

Arguing Against Hell From the Love of God

We hear it said often that God is too tender, kind and forgiving to allow men to suffer in Hell. Pleading the love and pity of God, men insist that He would not allow His creatures to perish. There are many beautiful and sentimental sayings about the love of God that are quoted to support the view that He would not allow one soul to suffer torment in eternity. But we dare never lose sight of the fact that one's escape from Hell is not dependent upon the love of God but upon the repentance and faith of each individual person. God is love, to be certain, but man also has a free will. Men are not doomed and damned to Hell by God, but they go there because they have willfully rejected God's only way of escape from sin's penalty, saving faith in the Lord Jesus Christ.

Hell—A Literal Place of Future Punishment

Some people engage themselves in much wishful thinking about Hell. It has been said that the fires of Hell mean the torments of conscience. Others say that Hell is simply the grave. We do not question that the torments of conscience will be included in the eternal punishment of the lost, though Hell will not be the torments of conscience only. But we cannot agree at all with those who teach that Hell is simply the grave. One must be either a deceiver or an illiterate to say that Hell is the grave. When the unsaved rich man died he went to Hell, and cried: "I am tormented in this flame" (Luke 16:24). Certainly he was not merely in the grave. He had five brothers whom he desired to be saved lest they also should come to that place of torment. Now if his five brothers would have repented and become saved, their conversion could not have kept them from the grave, for "it is appointed unto men once to die" (Hebrews 9:27). Hell is not the grave. The body of the rich man was dead, but that man knew that his soul was in a literal place and not merely in a spiritual state.

Will Future Punishment Be Endless?

At death the eternal state of each person is immutably fixed. The words "eternal," "everlasting," "for ever," and "for ever and ever" express endless duration. The New Testament use of these expressions denotes eternity. It is unreasonable to assume that there is an eternal Heaven but not an eternal

Hell. Eternal punishment is as much a truth of God's Word as is the eternal rewards for the righteous. The punishment of the wicked and the life of the righteous are for equal duration, "for ever and ever."

Where is Hell?

Here we cannot be dogmatic. This question cannot be answered fully. Geographically Hell cannot be located, for the Bible gives us no positive declarative statement of its situation. Where this outer darkness is, where the endless fire is, where Hell is we do not know, nor must we know. It is sufficient to say that Hell is a prepared place, and experientially it is at the end of every unsaved sinner's life.

CHAPTER NINE

Heaven—The Home of the Redeemed

Is it not strange that we do not take up the Bible to study more about the abode of the blessed dead who die in the Lord? Should not we ourselves become better acquainted with our future home? How dark would be the future if what we have been taught about Heaven were delusive and deceptive! But we can know the truth from God's Word and we can be certain that the descriptions of the Christian's future home are not fraudulent. Some years ago I was lured to an undesirable vacation spot by grossly exaggerated statements that spoke of refinement. Upon arriving I discovered that the town and its environment in no way tallied with the advertising. You can imagine how great was my disappointment. But the infallibility of the Holy Scriptures assures us of no disappointments in Heaven. We may be correctly informed by a careful study of what God says about it.

An instant after death the departed saint will know more about Heaven than all of the saints here on earth. But until we are called Home to be with the Lord, our knowledge is confined to what the Holy Spirit has revealed to us in the Bible.

There Is a Place Called Heaven

Some general ideas that are held about Heaven are not found in the Word of God. Because Heaven is beyond the limits of our vision many people regard it as merely a sphere of life, or a state independent of locality. But Heaven is a place. It was the dwelling *place* of Christ before His Incarnation. He said: "I came down from Heaven" (John 6:38). Heaven was also the place to which He ascended after His Resurrection. Luke says: "While He blessed them, He was parted from them, and carried up into Heaven" (Luke 24:51). It is the place where the glory and power of God are set forth. Jesus is there now, "set (or seated) on the right hand of the throne of the Majesty in the heavens" (Hebrews 8:1). Our Lord said: "I go to prepare a place for you" (John 14:2). When Jesus went away He must have gone somewhere, to a place. Therefore, we are not flattering ourselves with an unfounded hope that makes dying easier but that deceives us at the last. We believe in the Biblical Heaven as a definite, tangible place.

Where Is Heaven?

The Bible mentions three heavens: the aerial, the sidereal, and the celestial. First there is the atmospheric or aerial heavens where the birds fly. This is visible to the naked eye and is mentioned by Jeremiah where he said: "The birds of the heavens have fled" (Jeremiah 4:25). Next, there are the stellar or sidereal heavens from which shine the stars and constellations. Isaiah speaks of the Day of the Lord when "the stars of heaven and the constellations thereof shall not give their light" (Isaiah 13:10). Finally, there is the third Heaven, the celestial or "the Heaven of heavens" (2 Chronicles 6:18). "For Christ is not entered into the holy places made with hands, which are figures of the true; but into Heaven itself, now to appear in the presence of God for us" (Hebrews 9:24). Jesus said: "Let your light so shine before men, that they may see your good works and glorify your Father which is in Heaven" (Matthew 5:16). Here our Lord was referring to the third

Heaven, and He says the Father is there. When the believer dies he is "absent from the body, and present with the Lord" (2 Corinthians 5:8). He enters immediately into Heaven itself and is at home with the Lord.

Christians Are Citizens of Heaven

"For our citizenship is in Heaven; whence also we wait for a Saviour, the Lord Jesus Christ" (Philippians 3:20 R.V.). When Paul wrote this Epistle, Philippi was a Greek city but a colony of Rome, her citizens possessing Roman citizenship. The commonwealth of which the saints in Philippi were citizens had its fixed location in Rome. The Apostle Paul used this fact to illustrate to the believers their heavenly citizenship with its privileges and responsibilities. They were a heavenly people with a heavenly citizenship. Though they dwelt on earth, the commonwealth and the Sovereign of which the saints were citizens and subjects had its fixed location in Heaven. What was true of the saints at Philippi then is true of all believers. We were born from above. Ours is a heavenly destiny, and we are to live heavenly lives while we sojourn in a foreign land. As a heavenly people it is our privilege and responsibility to live a heavenly life on earth.

The Apostle Peter wrote: "Dearly beloved, I beseech you as *strangers* and *pilgrims,* abstain from fleshly lusts, which war against the soul" (1 Peter 2:11). As strangers and pilgrims we are living in a temporary dwelling beside natives of a foreign land. Jesus Christ is our Sovereign. One day He will come back for us and take us to our native Home, changing our bodies of humiliation like to the body of His glory. The curse of sin has humiliated these physical bodies of ours, but we are to abstain from fleshly lusts and live the same holy life here that we would were we at home in our native Land. The Christian has a temporary home in a territory ruled by Satan, but he is not to subject himself to the god of this world. We must remain true to our Sovereign, "considering the High Priest of our profession, Christ Jesus," for we have become "partakers of the heavenly calling" (Hebrews 3:1).

Is the Present Heaven the Final Abode of the Saints?

There are several verses of Scripture that have confused not a few students of the Bible on this question. The following verses have led some to believe that the earth and the heavens that now are will one day be annihilated.

"Of old hast thou laid the foundation of the earth: and the heavens are the work of thy hands. They shall perish, but thou shalt endure: yea, all of them shall wax old like a garment; as a vesture shalt thou change them, and they shall be changed" (Psalm 102:25, 26).

"And all the host of heaven shall be dissolved, and the heavens shall be rolled together as a scroll: and all their host shall fall down, as the leaf falleth off from the vine, and as a falling fig from the fig tree" (Isaiah 34:4).

"But the day of the Lord will come as a thief in the night; in the which the heavens shall pass away with a great noise, and the elements shall melt with fervent heat, and the earth also and the works that are therein shall be burned up. Seeing then that all these things shall be dissolved, what manner of persons ought ye to be in all holy conversation and godliness, Looking for and hasting unto the coming of the day of God, wherein the heavens being on fire shall be dissolved, and the elements shall melt with fervent heat? Nevertheless we, according to his promise, look for new heavens and a new earth, wherein dwelleth righteousness" (2 Peter 3:10-13).

"And the world passeth away, and the lust thereof: but he that doeth the will of God abideth for ever" (1 John 2:17).

"And I saw a great white throne, and him that sat on it, from whose face the earth and the heaven fled away; and there was found no place for them" (Revelation 20:11).

"And I saw a new heaven and a new earth: for the first heaven and the first earth were passed away; and there was no more sea" (Revelation 21:1).

From these inspired statements of Peter and John some have adopted the view that the present abode of the righteous dead is to be burned up, reduced to ashes, and an entirely new dwelling place created for all of the saved. The writer finds difficulty in reconciling this teaching with other Scriptures. The Psalmist testified: "Thy faithfulness is unto all generations: Thou hast established the earth, and it abideth" (Psalm 119:90). It is written: "One generation passeth away, and another generation cometh: but the earth abideth forever" (Ecclesiastes 1:4). Here the teaching appears to be that the creation of God will not be annihilated, for He has said that it abides forever. Is there a seeming contradiction? How can Heaven and earth be destroyed and yet abide forever?

After the Millennium and the final judgment of Satan the heavens and the earth will be thoroughly purged by fire. This does not mean that the old heavens and the old earth are to be completely consumed and reduced to ashes. Neither is there any indication that the new heaven and the new earth are to be entirely new planets. The old world probably will be destroyed by fire in the same sense that God destroyed it with water in Noah's day, "Whereby the world that then was, being overflowed with water, *perished*" (2 Peter 3:6). The world of Noah's day was not annihilated. Geologists agree to the fact that the present world shows evidence of being visited by a flood between five and six thousand years ago. When we read in Scripture that unbelievers shall "perish" (Luke 13:3, 5, 35), and be "destroyed" (Leviticus 23:30; Matthew 10:28), there is no thought of their being annihilated; for we have seen in two previous chapters how that both soul and body will exist in endless consciousness. But we do see an instructive parallel between the judgment of the earth by fire and the judgment of the lost by fire. Both are said to be "destroyed." Yet neither will be annihilated. We encounter no problem here when we think how the primitive earth which was made void by Satan (Genesis 1:2) was restored again by God and made new in the time of Adam and Eve.

It appears that the great conflagration, the flames and the melting, suggest the idea of purifying. There will be a new creation just as each believer who is born again is said to be a new creation. "Wherefore if any man is in Christ, he is a new creature (or a new creation): the old things are passed away: behold, they are become new" (2 Corinthians 5:17 R.V.). He is "created in Christ Jesus" (Ephesians 2:10). The new birth does not render inactive or annihilate the old nature. The child of God becomes a partaker of the New Nature which is divine, and all stain is purged by the Blood of Christ. Just exactly how God will bring to pass the purifying of the old heavens and the earth and make the new we do not know. But we are certain that they will pass through a molten ball of fire, and will come forth from that baptism of judicial fire clean and holy. Every stain of sin, every evidence of evil will be wiped out in that day.

We question the idea of the third Heaven being burned, for no purging or purifying is needed there. However, at the end of the day of the Lord, the earth and the heavens that surround it along with all the works of man will be consumed even as fire purifies gold. Then shall we have "a new heaven and a new earth" (Revelation 21:1)—not new in the sense of just coming into existence, but new in its renovation, transformation, and fixtures.

Our Home Over There

When our Lord was here upon earth, He said to His disciples: "I go to prepare a place for you" (John 14:2). He was thinking of His Death, Resurrection, and Ascension into Heaven itself in the presence of the Father. The dwelling of God always has been a stately abode. Jesus describes it as a place of "many mansions," one Heaven divided into many rooms. The desire of the heavenly Bridegroom is to make ready a room for each of His redeemed ones. This He has been doing, and it was the unique privilege of the Apostle John to get a glimpse of the final abode of the righteous. Since we have a divine revelation of our heavenly Home presented to us by the Holy Spirit, we are assured of the accuracy of every description that He has given.

John says: "I saw a new heaven and a new earth...the holy city, new Jerusalem, coming down from God out of heaven, prepared as a bride adorned for her husband" (Revelation 21:1, 2). We are being introduced here to a place of absolute perfection and of eternal immutability, the home of the saved of all ages. It is called "the holy city" (Revelation 21:2; 22:19), for in it every person and every thing will echo the glory and the holiness of God. All powers of evil and all unbelievers will have been cast into the lake of fire forever. This means that every possibility of sin will have been expelled. When Jesus said He was going to prepare a place for us, it would be just such a place as this that one would expect the holy Son of God, the divine Architect, to build. No mere mortal hands could be employed in the construction of the Holy City. It must be of heavenly origin and construction.

The fellowship in Heaven will surpass anything that we have known on earth. Up there "God is with men; He will dwell with them, and God Himself shall be with them." Men dwelling with *"God Himself"!* Could anything be higher and more glorious? Then we will know the blessed reality of the words of Christ, where He said: "Blessed are the pure in heart: for they shall see God" (Matthew 5:8). In addition to having fellowship with "God Himself," Father, Son and Holy Spirit, we will commune with the "innumerable company of angels, the general assembly and church of the firstborn, and to the spirits of just men made perfect" (Hebrews 12:22-24). What a fellowship! What a joy divine!

Heaven will bring permanent relief from all of the ills of earth. It is written of the redeemed that in Heaven "God shall wipe away all tears from their eyes." I have dried the tears of my own children many times, but I have discovered my inability to stop the tears. But God is able. And how our hearts yearn for the glad occasion when the loving and almighty hand of our heavenly Father shall wipe away, once for all, every tear. The tears that flow from "sorrow," "crying," and "pain" shall be dried forever, for these things are not known in the land of pure delight.

Heaven is revealed as a place of activity. John saw how that in the New Jerusalem "His servants shall serve Him" (Revelation 22:3). While it is true that Heaven is a place of rest, "a rest for the people of God," it will not be the rest of inactivity or idleness. Heaven would soon become monotonous if such were true. The saints "shall serve Him day and night in His temple" (Revelation 7:15), says John. By no means does the "rest" of the redeemed mean idleness. In Heaven we shall serve Him unhampered by earth's enemies and limitations, without painful stress and strain and sweat. In Heaven the joys and pleasures of our union with Jesus Christ will be appreciated and apprehended to the full, unhindered by the disturbing and distracting things on earth.

In Revelation 4:10, 11 we are clearly shown that in Heaven, we will worship our Lord and cast our crowns before His throne. On earth He is not worshipped and adored as He should be. Our so-called worship is sometimes no worship at all. How often we have gone through the motions when our hearts were not right! We enthrone self and steal the crowns to boast of what we have done. But yonder in the Land of pure delight, in our glorified state, we shall give Him our all.

How these thoughts of our future home and its varied spheres of activity should encourage us to more zealous and diligent service during earth's pilgrimage! There is much about our heavenly activity that we do not know in detail now, but in that day we shall know even as we are known. But we know that we shall be engaged with Him who has redeemed us and brought us to our eternal dwelling place.

Babies in Heaven?

Jesus said:

> "At the same time came the disciples unto Jesus, saying, Who is the greatest in the kingdom of heaven? And Jesus called a little child unto him, and set him in the midst of them, And said, Verily I say unto you, Except ye be converted, and become as little children, ye shall not enter into the kingdom of heaven. Whosoever therefore shall humble himself as this little child, the same is greatest in the kingdom of heaven" (Matthew 18:1-4).

> "Even so it is not the will of your Father which is in heaven, that one of these little ones should perish" (Matthew 18:14).

> "But Jesus said, Suffer little children, and forbid them not, to

come unto me: for of such is the kingdom of heaven" (Matthew 19:14).

Many able and well known Bible scholars have held the view that in Heaven there will be more occupants than in Hell. They base their belief on the fact that so many countless millions of children have died before reaching the age of accountability. It seems hardly possible that one of these little ones should ever be lost. Certainly they are not *saved*, that is, by believing in the Lord Jesus Christ (Acts 16:31). But it seems Scriptural and reasonable to conclude that all children who are not able to decide for themselves are divinely *safe*.

Christian parents should, by daily prayer, the reading of the Scriptures, church attendance, and an exemplary life seek to lead their children who have arrived at an age of accountability to a saving knowledge of the Lord Jesus Christ. The thought of my being in Heaven while my children are lost in Hell would make me tremble. Let us make our first aim and duty the salvation of our children so that in Heaven the family circle will be unbroken.

CHAPTER TEN

Shall We Know Each Other in Heaven?

Man is the acme of God's creation, the crown of all that our heavenly Father has brought into existence by His own mighty power. The remarkable strides that men have made in scientific research, in industrial progress, in agricultural development, and in the civilization and evangelization of the peoples of the world are an indication of the treasures of genius which God has put at man's disposal. Is it reasonable to believe "that He might lead it towards one place—a black hole in the ground where it could bury its intellect and memory and imagination and prayer in the depths with the leaf and the worm?"

The answer is "No." If death means the utter forgetfulness of God-given gifts and of earthly friends and loved ones in the Lord, then this aching emptiness in our hearts never shall be satisfied, and the undying memory of departed loved ones will never be anything more than just a buried hope.

The belief in recognition and reunion in the after life is a universal one. It prevailed among cultured philosophers and poets, among untutored pagans, and it is voiced by the peoples of the world in our own day. The universal, instinctive belief is that we shall know each other in the future life.

As we study the lives of Old Testament characters of whom it is said that they were gathered unto their people, we will find that it meant more than merely being buried with them. They were gathered to their loved ones in the abode of departed spirits with not one moment's solitude between their memories on earth and their joining them in Heaven. A blessed recognition! A hallowed reunion!

The attitude of David at the death of his child shows that Israel's King believed in Heavenly recognition. "I shall go to him" (2 Samuel 12:23). Would there be any comfort for David if he had to go to his child whom he would not know? What would the blind get out of going to behold the sunset? What would the deaf get out of going to hear music?

May we say here that we do not believe there will be infants in Heaven as such. There will be no deformed, deficient, nor decrepit bodies in Heaven. There will be no old age or infancy in the home of the blessed. However they will not appear in their resurrected bodies as infants, for, as Dr. West has said: "Infancy is an immature stage and an imperfect state of existence. Adam and Eve were not infants when made, but adults." We encounter no problem here in a parent recognizing its child in Heaven. When we think of Christian mothers who have died giving birth to a child, and the child growing to full maturity and becoming a Christian, we still believe that the mother shall recognize her son or daughter even though her last view of the child was in its infancy.

The scene on the Mount of Transfiguration is generally accepted as strong evidence of heavenly recognition. As Heaven shone forth in celestial effulgence, there appeared before Christ and His disciples Moses and Elijah. Not only were Moses and Elijah recognizable by our Lord, but they were known to the disciples also. When we recall how the disciples with earthly, limited vision could recognize the two saints from Heaven, certainly when we arrive there in our glorified bodies and with heavenly vision, we will be able to recognize those with whom we associated on earth.

When the rich man died and went to Hell, "he lift up his eyes, being in torments, and *seeth* Abraham afar off, and Lazarus in his bosom" (Luke 16:23). Here is a case that proves both recognition and remembrance in the future life. If, in the abode of the lost with its limitations of spiritual wisdom and perception, there is feeling for and recognition of loved ones, how much greater will be the affinity and knowledge of our loved ones in the eternal Home of the redeemed where cognizance is not limited!

Heaven is revealed as a social place, where enjoyment and fellowship are set forth under the figure of a feast. Jesus said: "And I say unto you, That many shall come from the east and west, and shall sit down with Abraham, and Isaac, and Jacob, in the kingdom of heaven" (Matthew 8:11). Assuredly the patriarchs and prophets knew each other at this holy festival, and so will the saved from every quarter of the earth.

The Apostle Paul believed and taught that Heaven was a place of mutual recognition for the children of God. In his first Epistle to the Thessalonians, Paul wrote: "For what is our hope, or joy, or crown of rejoicing? Are not even ye in the presence of our Lord Jesus Christ at His coming? For ye are our glory and joy" (1 Thessalonians 2:19, 20). There is no mistaking what Paul had in mind. He fully expected to meet the converts from Thessalonica in Heaven, and furthermore, he looked forward to being able to distinguish them from others who had found Christ during the years of his ministry.

Today our knowledge is confined to the revelation that God has given us, and how we do praise Him for that marvelous revelation in His Word! But in that day—"face to face"! O blessed hope! Face to face with family and friends whom we have loved and long since lost awhile. But more wonderful still: we shall see Him as He is, "face to face."